Labrador Retriever

By Nona Kilgore Bauer

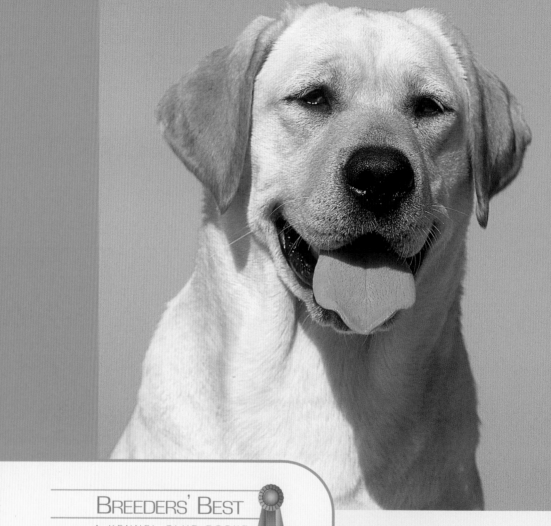

BREEDERS' BEST
A KENNEL CLUB BOOK™

LABRADOR RETRIEVER

ISBN: 1-59378-901-7

Copyright © 2004

Kennel Club Books, LLC
308 Main Street, Allenhurst, NJ 07711 USA
Printed in South Korea

10 9 8 7 6 5 4 3 2 1

PHOTOS BY:
Isabelle Français and
Bernd Brinkmann.

DRAWINGS BY:
Yolyanko el Habanero.

Contents

Meet the Labrador Retriever

Intelligent, affectionate, devoted to his owner. Talented and versatile, hunting upland game and waterfowl, yet content to share a couch cushion with a friend. Guide dog, assistance dog, therapy dog, drug and arson detector, search and rescue dog. Is it any wonder the Labrador Retriever has been America's most popular breed for more than a decade?

Wherever did this super-dog come from? Today's Labrador Retriever evolved from a hardy family of gundogs that were developed

The Labrador's instincts and skills as a retriever, especially in water, are prized traits in the breed that were developed and protected by the breed's founders.

during the early 1800s on the shores of Newfoundland (not Labrador!). As much at home in the water as on land, the Labrador Retriever frequently accompanied the Newfoundland fishermen on seafaring excursions.

LABRADOR HISTORY 101

Originally called the St. John's Dog or the Lesser Newfoundland, the Labrador Retriever first arrived in England in the 1820s. The English seamen and sportsmen bred these water-loving dogs to the English retriever types of that era. Those early gundog breeders had no idea that the future Labrador would ascend to the top of the canine world to become the most popular companion and sporting breed around the globe. Their sole intent was to develop a superb shooting dog that possessed strength of limb, scenting ability,

The lesser-known Flat-Coated Retriever is a relative of the Labrador. Although similar in looks, the Flat-Coat is of a lighter build and possesses a longer coat than the Lab.

The Chesapeake Bay Retriever shares its origins with the Labrador. The Chessie, also prized for its field abilities, has a dense, often wavy, coat and is seen in shades of brown.

CHAPTER 1

a smooth, easy-care coat fit for waterfowling and a love of water.

During the 1830s, the third Earl of Malmsbury (1807–1889) imported several of the dogs from Newfoundland. Malmsbury is credited with breeding true to type to preserve those qualities so valued in the Labrador Retriever. His determination was evident in a letter he wrote to the sixth Duke of Buccleuch. "We always call mine Labrador dogs and I have kept the breed as pure as I could from the first I had…"

Many other breeders of that era, who were not as selective as Malmsbury, crossed Labradors with other retrievers. Nearly always, the Labrador characteristics predominated in those matings, and their descendants were usually called Labradors. By the late 1800s, a predictable breed type had been established. Eventually Labrador Retriever fanciers

drew up a breed standard to discourage further crossings with other retrievers and to lock in the Labrador's structure and working ability.

The Labrador Retriever received official recognition from The Kennel Club of Great Britain in 1903, followed by American Kennel Club (AKC) acceptance in 1917. The breed received its real boost, however, from its success in the retriever field trials that were developed in the US during the 1930s by the various retriever breed clubs. In short order, both hunters and non-hunting dog lovers were smitten with the breed's working ability and pleasant personality. The Lab's unique combination of retrieving talent and trainability, "love-'em-all" disposition and easy-care coat made him an ideal candidate for other canine venues.

THE NUMBER-ONE DOG

For several decades, the Labrador Retriever numbered

among the ten most popular breeds registered with the AKC. In 1991, it climbed to the number-one spot, where it has American dog lovers. Highly intelligent, friendly and outgoing, eager to learn, good with kids and other pets and

With his outstanding scenting ability, agility and work ethic, as well as love of humans, the Labrador is used frequently to search for people trapped in collapsed buildings and other disaster sites.

continued to reign as America's favorite canine. In 2002, over 150,000 Labs were AKC-registered, more than twice as many as the second-place Golden Retriever. Field dog, show dog, working dog and family companion, the 21st-century Labrador Retriever is all that and more.

One look at the Labrador explains why this exceptional dog has captured the heart of sporting a drip-dry short coat…what's not to love?

Despite his metamorphosis into a "do-it-all" dog, the Labrador Retriever still reigns as the supreme upland game dog. His retrieving instincts, solidly imbedded during his rise to stardom, remain alive and well today, as evidenced by the vast numbers of family Labs who hunt all day and then curl up with their humans afterwards. He is a true outdoorsman who is blessed with boundless energy and enthusiasm. Whether hunting in the field or chasing Frisbees® in the back yard, the Lab dives into every activity with zest and gusto.

As the saying goes, "It ain't easy being number one!"

The Golden Retriever is a beautiful, talented and popular dog in his own right. This breed should not be mistaken for a longhaired yellow Lab, nor should a Lab be confused with his golden-coated cousin.

Seldom does a breed achieve such distinction without suffering deterioration in health or temperament, and the Lab is no exception. Capitalizing on breed popularity, irresponsible breeders and fanciers with little knowledge and experience have bred Labs with no concern for health or

true Lab temperament and ability. Today's Lab is more prone to the hereditary diseases that plague most retriever breeds. Hip and elbow dysplasia are commonplace and can cause debilitating arthritic changes. Progressive retinal atrophy and retinal dysplasia are serious eye problems that can result in complete loss of vision. Thyroid problems are common. All breeding stock should be screened and certified free of these problems before breeding. Buyers must search for reputable breeders and insist on seeing those clearances on the parents of the pup.

The male Labrador is a solid, muscular fellow who weighs 65 to 80 pounds and stands 22.5 to 24.5 inches at the shoulder. Females stand about an inch or 2 shorter and weigh about 10 pounds less. The breed's average lifespan is 11 to 14 years. The Labrador's short and tight coat comes in three colors: black, yellow and chocolate. Only these three colors are accepted by the AKC. The yellow coloration is called "yellow," not "golden." The word "golden" is associated with a completely different breed of dog, the Golden Retriever, a lovely sporting dog with a long, flowing coat. There are brindle Labradors, too, which are brown with black striations on the coat; they are not acceptable by any registry and therefore should not be considered true Labs.

Lab lovers will tell you that, whatever the coat color, there is no match for this breed! Life doesn't get any better than living with a Lab.

The Labrador Retriever is one of the breeds most widely used as guide dogs for the visually impaired.

MEET THE LABRADOR RETRIEVER

Overview

- The Labrador Retriever, known today as the world's "love 'em all, do it all" breed, originated from gundog breeds in Newfoundland.
- The Labrador was truly established as a breed in England, where sportsmen prized the Lab's hunting and retrieving skills on land and in water, as well as his friendly nature and easy-care waterproof coat.
- The third Earl of Malmsbury is noted for his selective breeding and preservation of true type in the breed, leading to the creation of a breed standard and official recognition.
- Once the Lab received AKC recognition in the US, it was full speed ahead. The breed captured the hearts of hunters and companion-dog fanciers alike, climbing to the top of the charts in popularity.

Description of the Labrador

The breed standard clearly defines the desired physical characteristics of the Labrador, which include the dog's being medium in size, strongly built, short-coupled, well balanced, athletic and well muscled.

Few breed standards capture the essence of their breed as does that of the Labrador Retriever. A standard is written by a breed's parent club and then approved by the American Kennel Club (AKC). It describes the ideal dog and provides a guideline for judging the dog in the show ring, as well as outlining a canine blueprint of sorts that breeders use to plan and develop breeding programs. Without such guidelines, all the qualities and abilities so valued in the Labrador could be diluted or lost completely.

Revised and approved in 1994, the Labrador standard places great emphasis on the Labrador Retriever's function in the field as well as his overall conformation. The standard leaves no doubt about this dog's role as an intelligent and efficient hunting dog. The parent club's determination to keep the "retriever" in the Labrador is obvious.

The Labrador Retriever is seen in black, yellow and chocolate, with wonderful personality and talents underneath, no matter the color.

The Lab is described as a sound and athletic performance animal, both physically and mentally. "The Labrador Retriever is a strongly built, medium-sized, short-coupled dog possessing a sound, athletic, well-balanced conformation that enables it to function as a retrieving gundog; the substance and soundness to hunt waterfowl or upland game for long hours under difficult conditions; the character and quality to win in the show ring; and the temperament to be a family companion." Well-

Of necessity, the Labrador must have a dense, weather-resistant coat for protection. This, coupled with his love of water and eagerness to please, makes a tireless worker, ideally suited to assisting the hunter under any conditions.

balanced certainly describes the Labrador!

"Physical features and mental characteristics should denote a dog bred to perform as an efficient retriever of game with a stable temperament for a variety of pursuits beyond the hunting environment." The Lab has surely proven his aptitude and merit in canine ventures in both sport and service to mankind.

"The most distinguishing characteristics of the Labrador Retriever are his short, dense, weather-resistant coat; an 'otter' tail; a clean-cut head with broad back skull and moderate stop; powerful jaws; and his 'kind' friendly eyes, expressing character, intelligence and good temperament. Above all, a Labrador Retriever must be well balanced, enabling him to move in the show ring or work in the field with little or no effort. The typical Labrador possesses style and quality without over-refinement, and substance without lumber or cloddiness.

The Labrador is bred primarily as a working gundog; structure and soundness are of great importance." Once again, the standard is emphatic about the Lab's role as a working gundog as well as his all-around good nature.

The standard further states the Labrador "shall be shown in working condition, well-muscled and without excess fat." Sections describing the Lab's structure, from neck to hindquarters, describe a muscular, athletic canine who is well equipped to spend the day afield.

Lab temperament is a hallmark of the breed. "The ideal disposition is one of a kindly, outgoing, tractable nature; eager to please and non-aggressive towards man or animal. The Labrador has much that appeals to people; his gentle ways, intelligence and adaptability make him an ideal dog."

This standard leaves no doubt about the ideal Labrador

Retriever. Unfortunately, today that "ideal" Lab is harder to find. Given the breed's unique combination of talent, trainability and kindly disposition, it has fallen victim to the whims of profit-seeking breeders, along with the preferences of hunters and show exhibitors who specialize in Labs for either show or field. Competitors breed and promote the type of dog that best suits their particular passion. Show dogs are bred primarily for those qualities that would bring a blue ribbon in the show ring, with not much concern for hunting ability. Breeders of the field dog focus on the qualities that would enhance the Lab afield, breeding dogs that are leaner, longer of leg and more animated.

In spite of this, the Lab has prevailed, right down to the companion Lab that may never see a mallard or a show ring. Most Labs still look and act like the traditional Labrador Retriever that adores the water and is obsessed with fetching sticks and socks. We can thank the third Earl of Malmsbury and his cohorts for that.

DESCRIPTION OF THE LABRADOR

Overview

- The breed standard for the Labrador is very emphatic in detailing the breed's skills and intended purpose as a hunting dog. All physical and temperamental characteristics result in a dog designed for long days in the field and/or water with his master.
- The Lab must be friendly, outgoing and tractable; an aggressive Lab is an oxymoron.
- Today's Lab has seen some division in type, as breeder preferences have resulted in "show-type" and "field-type" dogs.
- The standard set forth by the parent club stresses the all-around Lab, balanced in body and in mind and equally capable of bringing home downed game and blue ribbons.

CHAPTER 3

Are You a Labrador Person?

If there is one quality that defines the Labrador Retriever, it's an insatiable desire to retrieve. Labs love to fetch and carry something, *anything*, in their mouths. One cannot help but marvel at the breed's obsession with retrieving…if not a bird, then sticks and socks will do. You can usually identify a Labrador residence by the number of sticks and branches piled up at the back door! So don't blame your Lab when you can't find your shoes or

A look at this dog's friendly face shows why the breed has become so popular. Many a pet owner is attracted to the Labrador for his affable nature, loyalty, trainability and reputation as a gentle family dog.

socks. He can't help it! That compulsion to retrieve is in his genes.

Chewing is a natural by-product of retrieving, and Lab puppies are miniature chewing machines. Many chew their way well into adulthood, leaving telltale scars on their owners' furniture and woodwork. A wise owner can minimize this damage by providing appropriate chew toys and teaching the Lab puppy what he may and may not chew. Owners who fail to dog-proof their houses or supervise their puppies tell horror stories about the seemingly "indestructible" things that their Labs have consumed or destroyed. If you are not willing to train your pup and supervise him, be prepared to face the consequences.

Whether you are looking for a helper in the field or a swimming partner, you'll find a fellow water-lover in your Labrador.

The Lab is a highly social fellow and will not thrive without human contact and companionship. He is best suited to an active family that pursues activities that include their

The Labrador's acute scenting and tracking abilities are used frequently by police.

dog. He enjoys lively outdoor fun and games, which are excellent outlets for his energy and enthusiasm. Labs are as comfortable in water as they are on land, and swimming is their favorite sport (after retrieving, of course). Long walks once or twice a day are good for dog and human, providing exercise and quality time together and preventing your Lab from becoming bored or under-exercised, and thus destructive.

Labs are great with children, although Lab puppies can be especially exuberant, so both dog and kids must be supervised to prevent mishaps due to both parties' normal rowdiness.

The Lab is considered an "easy keeper," requiring minimal grooming and coat upkeep. They shed twice a year but drop a little hair all year long. Owners claim that Lab hair is magnetic and clings like glue to clothing and furniture. Neatniks should either relax their standards or think twice about living with a Lab.

Although the Lab excels in a variety of canine disciplines and competitions, he is known to want to do things "his way." He is as strong-willed as he is eager to please and thus can be somewhat difficult to train. Manners are best taught during puppyhood before you have 50 pounds of dog dragging you down the street!

Potential Lab owners should consider their intentions for their Lab before deciding on a dog and breeder. The split between field and show lines has created Labs with marked differences in temperament, structure and hunting ability. The field Lab who is bred for hunting is generally leaner and longer in leg, with a narrower skull and a higher energy level. The Lab who has been bred to win blue ribbons

If you like a versatile, active canine companion who will enjoy going with you to different places and participating with you in almost any activity, you may find that the Lab is the dog for you.

in the show ring is typically heavier boned, with shorter legs and a noticeably broader skull. The show Lab is more laid-back and less intense in the field. Decide what you are looking for in your Lab companion before you go shopping for a breeder.

That being said, even a show-bred Lab puppy can be a handful. His enthusiasm and zest for life can easily overwhelm a novice owner

while highly trainable, the Lab still requires training. He is more than anxious to please his people, but he needs to learn how to do that. Obedience training is the commonsense route to transforming a "wild and crazy" Lab into a well-behaved, happy canine good citizen.

Labrador rescue groups (breed organizations that re-home abandoned Labradors) routinely deal with disen-

Lab owners must make plenty of provisions for their orally fixated retrievers' safe chewing.

who is unprepared for the breed's natural vigor and vitality. Perhaps due to the breed's high profile, many Lab owners are unaware that,

chanted owners who give up their Labradors because of temperament and behavior problems. Most likely, these dogs were never trained or poorly trained at best. Fortunately, many stout-hearted Lab owners who fail to train their dogs learn to tolerate and adjust to their Labs' wild and unruly ways because they love their dogs. Nevertheless, proper training is the best answer with any dog, especially one as big and bold as the Lab.

Breed selection is a weighty decision and should be based on what's best for both you and the dog. All this and more should determine whether or not you and a Labrador Retriever are meant to live happily ever after.

Healthy, sound puppies start with meticulously planned breeding, using only dogs who have been cleared of genetic problems and who will pass on the best qualities of the breed to the next generation.

ARE YOU A LABRADOR PERSON?

Overview

- The first thing that a Lab owner must understand is the breed's oral fixation. Providing chew toys, dog-proofing the home and training the dog what not to chew are essential elements in developing a companion dog with whom you are able to live happily.
- The Lab loves his people and needs to be included with his family.
- Great with kids, low-maintenance in terms of grooming, friendly and versatile, the Lab offers many wonderful pet qualities.
- Labs, especially as puppies, can get a little crazy! Owners must commit themselves to training, as this means the difference between an enjoyable companion and an uncontrollable nuisance.
- Look beyond the breed's popularity and widespread appeal to determine if the Lab really is the right dog for you, and vice versa!

Selecting a Breeder

A Labrador Retriever breeder should not be difficult to find, considering the vast number of breeders who produce those many thousands of Lab pups every year. But finding a *great* breeder, which is what you want, may not be quite as easy. Whatever your reasons for wanting a Labrador, hunting, dog shows, obedience, other types of competition or "just a nice pet," you want a healthy dog with a good disposition and correct Labrador instincts. Otherwise, why get a Labrador? Finding a

Are you dreaming of an adorable bundle of Labrador puppy love in your life? Read on, then, and arm yourself with the tools you'll need to make a wise and informed choice.

reputable, ethical breeder whom you can trust, who has experience with the breed and raises quality Lab puppies, may take time, but a sound and healthy pup is worth the extra effort.

Searching for a breeder and puppy can be an emotionally trying experience, taxing your patience and your willpower. All puppies are adorable, and it's easy to fall in love with the first cute pup you see. But a poor-quality Labrador will have health and temperament problems that can empty your wallet and break your heart. So do your breeder homework before you visit those cute pups. Arm yourself with a list of questions for the breeder. Then leave your wallet and your kids at home so you aren't tempted to take home a poorly bred but nonetheless irresistible Lab pup.

A dog show where the Labrador is being exhibited is a good place to meet people in the breed. Remember that type varies, so observe the dogs and introduce yourself to the handlers of the dogs you like after they are finished showing.

If you are looking for a field dog, you will want to locate a breeder who is active with his dogs in hunting and related pursuits.

PEDIGREE AND REGISTRATION

For starters, always ask to see the litter's pedigrees and registration papers. Although AKC registration is no guarantee of quality, it is one small step in the right direction. And if you hope to show your pup or enter licensed competitions, registration with the AKC is necessary.

The pedigree should include three to five generations of ancestry. Inquire about any titles in the pedigree. Titles simply indicate a dog's accomplishments in some area of canine competition, thus proving the merits of the ancestors and adding to the breeder's credibility. You may see "Ch." for a championship in conformation, "FC" for Field Champion or "OTCh." for Obedience Champion. A Lab that has two or three of these may be referred to as a Dual Champion or Triple Champion. These are rare but do exist in this very talented breed. While it is true that, like the registration, a pedigree cannot guarantee

health or good temperament, a well-constructed pedigree is still a good insurance policy and a good starting point.

There should be no extra fee, by the way, for either the pedigree or registration papers. The AKC states that papers do not cost extra, and any breeder who charges for these documents is unscrupulous.

WHY THIS BREEDING?
It's fine to ask the breeder questions, including one as simple as "Why did you choose to breed these two dogs together?" A conscientious breeder plans a litter of Labradors for specific reasons and should explain the genetics behind this particular breeding and what he expects the breeding to produce. In a breed like the Labrador, it's best to avoid the hobby breeder, meaning someone who has a couple of dogs and just mates the two together because they're both such

The Orthopedic Foundation for Animals (OFA) was founded by John M. Olin and a group of caring veterinarians and dog breeders in the mid-1960s. The goal of the foundation was to provide x-ray evaluations and guidance to dog breeders with regard to hip dysplasia, a common hereditary disease that affects many different breeds of dog.

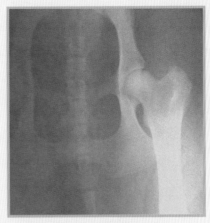

X-ray of a dog with "Good" hips.

Three board-certified OFA radiologists evaluate x-rays of dogs that are 24 months of age or older, scoring their hips as "Excellent," "Good" or "Fair," all of which are eligible for breeding. Dogs that score "Borderline," "Mild," "Moderate" and "Severe" are not eligible for breeding. The sire and dam of your new puppy should have OFA numbers, proving that they are eligible for breeding.

Since the OFA's inception, the organization has expanded to include databases on elbow dysplasia, patellar luxation, autoimmune thyroiditis, congenital heart disease, Legg-Calve-Perthes disease, sebaceous adenitis, congenital deafness, craniomandibular osteopathy, von Willebrand's disease, copper toxicosis, cystinuria, renal dysplasia and other diseases that have hereditary bases in dogs.

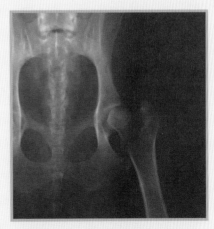

X-ray of a dog with "Moderate" dysplastic hips.

Visit the OFA website for more information on the organization, its history, its goals and the diseases from which it safeguards our pure-bred dogs. Go to *www.offa.com*.

"perfect pets." Regardless of how nice these dogs are, the chances of their being ideal for mating purposes is slim, especially given the many hereditary problems known in the breed.

HEALTH MATTERS

This brings us to the discussion of health issues and clearances. Labradors are prone to hip and elbow dysplasia and osteochondritis dissecans (OCD), three hereditary and potentially crippling joint diseases. Do the sire and dam have hip and elbow clearances from the OFA (Orthopedic Foundation for Animals, a national genetic-disease screening organization)? Have the parents' eyes been examined for progressive retinal atrophy (PRA) and cataracts within the past year by a board-certified veterinary ophthalmologist? Eye clearances can be registered with the Canine Eye Registry Foundation (CERF).

Good breeders will gladly, in fact proudly, provide documentation of the necessary health testing and clearances.

Other health problems recognized in the Labrador Retriever include epilepsy and, in some field lines, exercise-induced collapse (EIC), a condition in which dogs become weak and collapse shortly after mild to moderate exercise. You can research these and other Lab health problems on the breed parent club's website at *www.thelabradorclub.com* or research canine health websites.

BREED ACTIVITIES

Experienced Labrador breeders are frequently involved in some aspect of the dog fancy with their dog(s), perhaps showing in conformation, hunt tests or field trials, or training them for other performance events or dog-related activities. Their

Lab(s) may have earned titles in various competitions, which is added proof of these breeders' experience and commitment to the breed.

If you find a breeder who has no interest whatsoever in the dog sport, you most likely should keep shopping. Dog shows, field and obedience trials and hunt tests are all designed to determine which dog is the best of the best, and only proven winners should be selected to produce the next generation of Labs.

BREED CLUBS

Dedicated breeders often belong to The Labrador Retriever Club, Inc., and/or a local breed or kennel club. Such affiliation with other experienced breeders and sportsmen expands their knowledge of their chosen breed, which further enhances their credibility. Responsible breeders, by the way, do not raise several different breeds of dog or produce multiple litters of pups throughout the year. One or two litters a year is typical.

THE BREEDER'S QUESTIONS FOR YOU

The breeder will ask you questions, too, about your dog

A Labrador breeder should be a true Labrador lover! She of course should keep Labs of her own and should be active with her dogs, appreciating the wonderful qualities that make the breed so special.

history, such as previous dogs you have owned, which breed(s) of dog and what became of those dogs. He will want to know your living arrangements, i.e., house, yard, kids, other pets, etc., your goals for the pup and how you plan to raise the pup. His primary concern is the future of his puppies and whether you and your family are suitable owners who will provide a proper and loving home for his little one. You should be suspicious of any breeder who agrees to sell you a Lab puppy without any type of interrogation or interview process. Such indifference indicates the breeder's lack of concern about his pups and casts doubt on the breeder's ethics and his breeding program.

PROS AND CONS

A good breeder also will warn you about the downside of the Labrador. No breed of dog is perfect, nor is every breed suitable for every person's temperament and lifestyle. Be prepared to weigh the bad news with the good about the Lab. While we have waxed poetic about the Lab's many fine attributes, the breed does have some drawbacks. Labradors shed and can have a doggy odor. They are rather

big dogs with lots of energy to channel, more than many owners can handle or know what to do with. Labs require a lot of attention and will not do well if left alone home all day with no stimulation or inter-action with people.

SALES CONTRACT

Most reputable breeders have a puppy sales contract that includes specific health guarantees and reasonable return policies. The breeder should agree to accept a puppy back if things do not work out. He also should be willing, indeed anxious, to check up on the puppy's progress after the pup leaves for his new home. The breeder also should be available to help if you have questions or problems with the pup.

AKC ILP

Many breeders place their pet-quality puppies on the AKC's Indefinite Listing Privilege (ILP). This does register pups with the AKC and allows dog and owner to compete in AKC-licensed companion and performance events (not conformation or field trials), but does not allow American Kennel Club registration of any offspring from the mature dog. The purpose of ILP is to prevent indiscrim- inate breeding of "pet-quality" Labrador Retrievers. The breeder, and only the breeder, can cancel this limited regis- tration if the adult dog develops into breeding quality.

A breeder may specialize in a certain coat color or may breed for all three. Regardless, his love of the Labrador and the best interests of the breed should be the foremost ingredients in his breeding program.

unlikely that a breeder will offer names of unhappy puppy clients, but calling other owners of the breeder's dogs may make you more comfortable dealing with that particular breeder.

REFERENCES

If you have any doubts at all, feel free to ask for references and check with them. It's

BREEDER REFERRALS

Check with the American Kennel Club for breeder referrals in your area. The AKC website *(www.akc.org)* offers links to Labrador breed clubs

CHAPTER 4

and breeders throughout the United States. The Labrador Retriever Club's website also is an excellent source for beeder referrals, listing contact information for their member breeders, who are obliged to uphold the club's Code of Ethics in their breeding programs. Call and ask about their litters. Any information gleaned from these conversations will make you a smarter shopper when you visit a litter of pups.

COST
You can expect to pay a dear price for all of these breeder qualities, whether you purchase a Labrador as a companion dog or one with show or working potential. Many breeders evaluate their puppies, and those with little or no show potential are considered "pet quality" and sold for less than their show- or field-potential pups. "Pet quality," of course, does not mean unsound or atypical. A pet must be as healthy and sound as any top show or working dog, and the pet Lab should look and act like a true Labrador Retriever. The discount or bargain Lab is not a bargain at all. Indeed, the discount pup is in reality a potential disaster that has little chance of developing into a healthy, stable adult. Such "bargains" could ultimately cost you a fortune in vet expenses and heartache that can't be measured in dollars and cents.

WHERE (AND WHERE *NOT*) TO LOOK
How do you find a reputable breeder whom you can trust? Do your homework before you visit puppies. Research the breed and make contact with experienced breed folk. Spend the day at a dog show or another dog event where you can meet breeders and handlers and get to know their dogs. Most Labrador devotees are more than happy to show off their dogs and brag about their accomplishments. If you know a Lab of whom you are fond,

ask the owner where the dog came from and then research the source.

Where not to look for your Lab puppy? Skip the puppy ads in your local newspaper. Reputable breeders rarely advertise in newspapers. They are very particular about prospective puppy owners and do not rely on mass advertising to attract the right people. Instead, they depend on referrals from other breeders and previous puppy clients.

They are more than willing to keep any puppy past the usual eight-week placement age until the right person comes along.

WORTH THE WAIT
Perhaps the second most important ingredient in your breeder search is patience. You will not likely find the right breeder or litter on your first go-around. Good breeders often have waiting lists, but a good Labrador pup is worth the wait.

SELECTING A BREEDER

Overview

- In a breed as popular as the Labrador, there are many profit-seeking, less-than-ethical breeders. You must find a good breeder who is devoted to the Labrador Retriever's best interests.
- Ask to see the pup's pedigree and registration papers, and be sure to ask many questions of the breeder, especially about the background and health of the litter's parents.
- The Labrador Retriever Club, Inc. is a trusted breeder referral. Membership shows that a breeder is truly involved in the breed and is committed to following strict breeding rules as set forth by the club.
- Expect the breeder to interview you, too! He wants to make sure that you are a fit owner, just as you want to make sure that he is a reputable breeder.

CHAPTER 5

Finding the Right Puppy

A good breeder does more than produce quality puppies. He will also evaluate the litter and help his clients find the pup that will best suit their needs and lifestyle. Picking the right puppy is a key component to a happy future with your pet.

You may have to put on your traveling shoes, as the perfect puppy is seldom right around the corner. Be willing to travel to visit any litter of pups you are considering; if possible, visit more than one breeder and litter. You will be surprised at the differences from one litter to the next. You'll be a smarter shopper for your efforts and thus end

Yes, black pups can be born to yellow parents! Breeders spend much time researching color genetics so that they know what to expect from each particular mating.

up with a better pup.

A visit to the litter involves much more than puppy hugs and kisses. It's more like your ultimate job interview. While searching for your new Labrador family member, you'll be checking out the applicants: the puppies, their parents and the breeder, as well as the living environment in which the pups are raised.

Which color puppy will you choose? Each color in the Lab is as appealing as the next, in a solid shade with beautiful sheen.

Where and how a litter of pups is raised is vitally important to the pups' early development into confident and social animals. The litter should be kept indoors, in the house or in an adjoining sheltered area, not isolated in a basement, garage or outside kennel building. A few experienced breeders sometimes have separate breeding facilities for their litters. You will know that you have found an exceptional breeder when you see the walls lined with blue ribbons and dozens of champion certificates.

Peekaboo! Popping out to steal your heart is an adorable yellow trio.

Wherever their living quarters, Lab puppies need to be socialized daily with people and people activities. The greater the pups' exposure to household sights and sounds between three to four weeks and seven weeks of age, the easier their adjustment will be to their future human families..

During your visit, scrutinize the puppies as well as their living areas for cleanliness and signs of sickness or poor health. The pups should be reasonably clean (allowing for normal non-stop "puppy-pies"). They should appear energetic, bright-eyed and alert. Healthy pups have clean, thick coats, are well proportioned and feel solid and muscular without being overly fat and pot-bellied. Watch for crusted eyes or noses and any watery discharge from the noses, eyes or ears. Listen for coughing or mucousy sniffing or snorting. Check for evidence of watery or bloody stools, of which there should be none.

Visit with the dam and the sire if possible. In many cases, the sire is not on the premises, but the breeder should at least have photos, his pedigree and a resume of his characteristics and accomplishments. It is normal for some dams to be somewhat protective of their young, but overly aggressive behavior is unacceptable. Labrador Retrievers are among the friendliest of creatures, and it's a rare Lab that will shy away from a friendly overture. Temperament is inherited, and if one or both parents are aggressive or very shy, it is likely that some of the pups will inherit those atypical characteristics.

It's also normal for a new dam to have a rather scrawny coat or be on the thin side after weeks of nursing hungry pups. However, there is an obvious difference between normal post-partum appearance and signs of poor health or neglect.

Notice how the pups interact with their littermates

and their surroundings, especially their response to people. They should be active and outgoing. In most Lab litters, some pups will be more outgoing than others, but even a quiet pup that is properly socialized should not be shy or spooky or shrink from a friendly voice or outstretched hand.

The breeder should be honest in discussing any differences in puppy person-alities. Although many breeders do some sort of temperament testing, they also have spent most of the past seven or eight weeks cuddling and cleaning up after these pups and by now know the subtle differences in each pup's personality. The breeder's observations are valuable aids in selecting the Labrador puppy that is right for

you and your lifestyle.

Tell the breeder if you plan to show your pup in confor-mation, hunt with your dog or compete in performance events or Lab-related activities. Some pups will show more promise

A good-quality pup doesn't just sprout up in the garden! You will need to look much farther than your back yard to find an ethical, responsible breeder with the pup that will be your perfect match.

than others for certain pursuits, and the breeder can help you select one that will best suit your long-term goals.

LET'S TALK ABOUT SEX

Do you prefer a male or female? Which one is right for you? Both sexes are loving and loyal, and the differences are due more to individual personality traits rather than to gender. The adult Labrador female is a lovable girl who is easy to live with. But she also can be a bit more moody, depending on her whims and hormonal peaks.

The adult male is often up to 2 inches taller than the female and is heavier boned, weighing 65 to 80 pounds. Although males tend to be more even-tempered than bitches, they are also more physical and exuberant during adolescence, which can be problematic in a large and powerful dog. An untrained male can also become dominant with people and other dogs. A solid foundation in obedience is necessary if you want your Lab pup to respect you as his leader.

Intact males tend to be more territorial, especially with other male dogs. In male puppies, both testicles should be descended into the scrotum. A dog with undescended testicles will make a fine pet but will be ineligible to compete in the show ring.

The spay/neuter process creates a level playing field and eliminates most of the behavioral differences. Your Lab will live longer, too, as the procedure offers many health benefits. For pups not of breeding quality, good breeders will require you to sign a spay/neuter agreement, obliging you to have this done at the proper age.

BEFORE YOU GO HOME

By eight weeks of age, when it's time to leave for new homes, the pups should have had at least one worming and a first puppy shot, and have vet's certificates verifying their good health at the time of the exam. Some Labrador breeders feel that separating the vaccines in a puppy's first shots reduces the possibility of negative reactions to the various components in the combination vaccines. Ask your breeder and your veterinarian for their recommendations on a safe vaccination program.

The breeder should tell you what the pup has been eating, when and how much. Some send home a small supply of puppy food to mix with your own for the first few days. Most breeders also give their clients a puppy "take-home" packet, which includes a copy of the pup's health certificate and records, the puppy's pedigree and registration papers, copies of the parents' clearances and the breeder's sales contract if he has one. Many supply literature on the breed and how to properly raise a Labrador pup. Dedicated breeders know that the more you know, the better the life ahead for their precious Lab pups. Your goal should be to find one of those breeders.

FINDING THE RIGHT PUPPY

Overview

- You must use your head in your selection; don't just lose your heart and pick the first puppy you see!
- Visiting the litter enables you to see where the pups have been raised, meet the puppies' mother and verify that all pups are in good health.
- During your puppy visit, you will get a taste of each pup's personality, thus helping you to decide which one appeals to you most. You can't make the choice based on looks alone.
- Do you prefer a male or female? Do you prefer a certain coat color? Do you have intentions to show, hunt or compete with your Lab? These considerations all must be discussed with the breeder so that he can steer you in the right direction.
- Along with your puppy, be sure to get all relevant documentation from the breeder.

CHAPTER 6

Welcoming the Lab Puppy

You need to prepare your home and family for the pup's arrival. Purchase all of your puppy supplies, then do a thorough check to make sure your home is safe for your puppy indoors and out (and that your house is safe from the pup!). Do the puppy-proofing *before* your pup comes home. Believe me, you won't have much time after he arrives.

It's a big world out there for a small pup! You must create a safe environment indoors and out for your puppy to be secure and comfortable in his new home.

SHOPPING SPREE

Shopping for puppy supplies is the fun part, but the non-essentials are often too cute to resist! "Stocking up" can easily decimate your budget, so start with basic essentials and save the puppy goodies until later.

Food and water bowls: You'll need two separate serving pieces, one for food and one for water. Stainless steel pans are your best choice, as they are lightweight, chew-proof and easy to clean. Tip-proof is a good idea, too, since most puppies love to splash about in their water bowls and the Labrador is the epitome of a water-loving pup.

As a pup, your Labrador will need only small bowls. As he gets bigger, you will need bigger bowls. A topic of debate is whether or not elevated bowls are healthier for the adult Lab; discuss this with your vet.

Puppy food: Your Lab puppy should be fed a quality food that is appropriate for his age and breed. Most quality dog foods now offer breed-specific formulas that address the nutritional needs of small, medium and large (your Labrador) breeds of dog during the various stages of their lives. Large-breed growth food should be his diet for his first year. After that, you can switch to a large-breed adult maintenance food.

Toys, toys, toys! You can't have enough for this insatiable chewer. Have a supply of toys on hand, but only offer a few at a time or else he will become spoiled and picky about which toys he uses.

Crate: A crate is your most valuable tool for housebreaking your pup, and his favorite place to feel secure. Crates come in wire mesh, fabric mesh and the familiar plastic airline-type varieties. Wire- or fabric-mesh crates offer the best ventilation, and some conveniently fold up suitcase-style. A fabric-mesh

Labrador Retrievers welcome space for free running and playing. A securely fenced yard is necessary, and don't under-estimate the dog's ability to dig, climb and jump when installing a fence to truly contain your Labrador.

crate might be a little risky for the youngster who likes to dig and chew.

Whatever your choice, purchase a large adult-sized crate rather than a small or puppy size; your Lab will soon grow into it. Crates are available at most pet stores and through pet-supply catalogs.

Collar and ID tag: Your Lab pup should have an adjustable collar that expands to fit him as he grows. Lightweight nylon adjustable collars work best for both pups and adult dogs. Put the collar on as soon as your pup comes home so he can get used to wearing it. The ID tag should have your phone number, name and address, but not the puppy's name, as that would enable a stranger to identify and call your dog. Some owners include a line that says "Dog needs medication" to hopefully speed the dog's return if he is lost or stolen. Attach the tag with an "O" ring (the kind used in key rings), as the more common "S" ring snags on carpets and comes off easily.

Today, even dog collars have gone high-tech. Some come equipped with beepers and tracking devices. The most advanced pet identification tool uses a Global Positioning System and fits inside a collar or tag. When your dog leaves his programed home perimeter, the device sends a message directly to your phone or email address.

Choke collars and pinch collars are for training purposes and should be worn only during training sessions. These training collars should never be used on Lab puppies under 16 weeks of age.

Leashes: For your puppy's safety and your own convenience, his leash wardrobe should include at least two kinds of leads. A narrow six-foot leather or nylon leash is best for house-training, puppy kindergarten and obedience classes and leash training.

Also consider a flexible lead. This is an extendable lead housed in a large handle, and it extends and retracts with the push of a button. This is the ideal tool for exercising puppies and adult dogs and should be a staple in every leash-trained Lab's wardrobe. Flexible leads are available in different lengths (8 feet to 26 feet) and strengths,

A wire crate of ample size for an adult Labrador is one of your most important purchases, as it will be your dog's "home within a home" for his entire life.

depending on breed size. Longer is better, as it allows your dog to run about and check out the good sniffing areas farther away from you. These leads are especially handy for exercising your Lab in unfenced areas or when traveling with your dog. You are wise to heel-train your puppy before he gets used to running amok on a flexible lead.

Gate: A well-placed baby gate will keep puppy safe, protect your house from the inevitable puppy mischief and thus save your sanity as well. It's wise to confine the puppy to a tiled or uncarpeted room or space, one that is accessible to the outside door that he will use for potty trips. Gated to a safe area where he cannot wreak havoc or destruction, the puppy will soon master the house-breaking routine, chew only appropriate chew toys rather than your antique furniture and spare himself unnecessary corrections for normal puppy mishaps.

Gated, however, does not mean unsupervised. Labs bore easily and have been known to entertain themselves by chewing through doors and drywall. If your puppy must be unattended, use his crate.

Bedding: Dog beds are just plain fun. However, don't go crazy just yet. Better to save that fancy bed for when your Labrador is older and less likely to shred it up or make a puddle on it. For puppy bedding, it's best to use a large towel, mat or blanket that can be easily laundered (which will probably be often).

Grooming tools: Labs are considered "easy keepers." You don't need a battery of combs and brushes to keep them tidy. A slicker brush and a grooming glove are the only implements needed to maintain a clean and shiny coat. Introduce your puppy to grooming with a soft bristle brush early on so he learns to like the process. It also helps condition the pup to hands-on attention, which will be invaluable when you have to clean his teeth and ears and clip his nails.

Toys: Puppies, especially oral breeds like the Lab, love all sorts of fuzzy toys that they can fetch and carry about. Many pups will snuggle with their woolly toys as they would their littermates. Eventually, though, most puppies shred their fuzzy toys, which is your cue to remove them and no longer buy them.

Of course, retrieving toys are a must for Labradors. Fetching and carrying will be two of his favorite things to do. Safe chew objects are a must if you hope to direct your Lab's chewing to acceptable objects and away from your shoes and furniture. Hard sterilized plastic bones are excellent "chewcifiers" and come in age-appropriate sizes.

Old shoes, socks and slippers are off limits, since even a smart pup can't distinguish his stuff from your own. Also avoid soft, squishy rubber toys or ones with button eyes or "squeakers" that could be swallowed in a blink.

One important puppy toy rule: offer only two or three toys at a time. If you give your puppy a smorgasbord of toys, he will soon become bored with all of them and look for more. Select only one toy at a time to put in the crate with him.

PUPPY-PROOFING

After puppy shopping, you must puppy-proof your house. Folks who fail to puppy-proof can tell you horror stories! Labrador pups are naturally curious critters that will investigate everything new, then seek-and-destroy just because it's fun. *Never* let your puppy roam your house unsupervised.

Scout your house for the following potentially hazardous

Puppy-proofing is just as important outdoors; remember your Lab's oral tendencies! Be sure that no toxic plants or flowers are in any areas to which the dog has access, and do not use gardening chemicals, fertilizers or anything else that could be harmful.

items and remove them from your Lab's reach. The kitchen garbage can (and the diaper pail, if you still have un-house-broken children) is a natural puppy magnet. Remember how terrific the dog's nose is—about 50,000 times more sensitive than your own. Just imagine how these things smell to your Lab puppy. Gather any medication bottles, cleaning

Socialization is fun for all! Everyone you meet will delight in making the acquaintance of a friendly Labrador youngster.

materials and roach and rodent poisons from around the house. Lock these up. You'll be amazed at what a determined puppy can find. Unplug electrical cords and other wires wherever you can and make the others inaccessible. Injuries from chewed electrical cords are

extremely common in young dogs. Beware of fertilizers, chemicals and especially antifreeze! It is extremely toxic and even a few drops will kill a dog of any age and size.

Some less obvious items that can tie your puppy up are dental floss, yarn, needles and thread and other stringy stuff. Puppies snuffling about at ground level will find and ingest the tiniest of objects and will end up in surgery. Most vets will gladly tell you stories about the stuff they've surgically removed from puppies' guts.

Another hazard is toilet bowl cleaners, which make the water in the bowl look blue-green or some other unnatural color. No matter how nice they smell, you must discard them. All dogs are born with toilet sonar and quickly discover that the water there is always cold. Green water is never good!

Just like your mother used to nag you about, puppy owners must keep their socks, underwear, shoes and slippers off the floor and in their proper places. Don't forget to close your closet doors. Puppies love all of these things because they smell like their favorite people!

The bottom line with puppy-proofing is that you must be on your toes—always be a few steps ahead of your "nosy" Labrador. Use common sense and you and your Labrador puppy will enjoy a happy and safe home life together.

SOCIALIZATION

This actually puppy-proofs your puppy, not your house. Puppy socialization is your Lab's insurance policy to a happy, stable adulthood, and is, without question, the most important element in a Lab puppy's introduction to the human world. Although Labs are by nature outgoing and gregarious dogs, it is still most important to expose them to strangers and new situations at an early age. Unsocialized pups grow up to be spooky and insecure and fearful of people, children and strange places. Many turn into fear biters or become aggressive with other dogs, strangers, even family members. Such dogs can seldom be rehabilitated and often end up abandoned in animal shelters where unfortunately they are eventually euthanized. Puppy socialization lays the foundation for a well-behaved adult canine, thus preventing these sad scenarios.

A canine's primary socialization period occurs during the puppy's first 20 weeks of life. Once he leaves the safety of his mom and littermates at eight to ten weeks of age, your job begins. Start with a quiet, uncomplicated household for the first day or two, then gradually introduce him to the sights and sounds of his new human world. Frequent interaction with children, new people and other dogs is essential at this age. Visit new places (dog-friendly, of course) like parks or even the local grocery-store parking lot where there are crowds of people. Set a goal of two new places a week for the next two months. Keep these new situations upbeat and positive, which will create a positive attitude toward future encounters.

Labrador Retrievers are exceptional family pets and good with children, but the relationship must be nurtured from the beginning so that child and dog behave properly with each other.

"Positive" is especially important when visiting your veterinarian. You don't want a pup that quakes with fear every time he sets a paw inside his doctor's office. Make sure your vet is a true dog lover as well as a good dog doctor.

Your puppy also will need supervised exposure to children. Puppies of all breeds tend to view little people like toddlers and small children as littermates and will attempt to

exert the upper paw (a dominance ploy) over the child. Because he was bred to hunt and carry game, a Lab pup is very oral and will mouth a child's fingers and toes. Adult family members should supervise and teach the puppy not to bite or jump on the kids.

Although Labs are generally good with children, they are happy, enthusiastic dogs that could unintentionally overwhelm a small child during play. Both dog and child must be taught how to play properly with each other, and children must learn to respect their puppy's privacy and handle him with care. Teach the children not to run or otherwise entice the puppy into rambunctious behavior that could lead to unnecessary corrections for the pup.

Take your Lab youngster to puppy school. Some classes accept pups from 10 to 12 weeks of age, with one series of puppy shots as a health requirement. The younger the pup, the easier it is to shape good behavior patterns. A good puppy class teaches proper canine social etiquette rather than rigid obedience skills. Your puppy will meet and play with young dogs of other breeds, and you will learn about the positive teaching tools you'll need to train your pup. Puppy class is important for both novice and experienced puppy folks. If you're a smart Lab owner, you won't stop there and will continue on with a basic obedience class.

Remember this: there is a direct correlation between the quality and amount of time you spend with your puppy during his first 20 weeks of life and the character of the adult dog he will become. You cannot recapture this valuable learning period, so make the most of it.

WELCOMING THE LAB PUPPY

Overview

- You should obtain all of the necessary accessories for your pup before bringing him home. Safe chew toys are especially important for a mouthy young Lab.
- Also before the pup comes home, you must puppy-proof your home and yard to create a safe, hazard-free environment. Puppy-proofing protects both your pup and your house!
- Once your pup is used to his new home, you can begin to welcome him into the world around him. Socializing the pup by allowing him to meet new people, interact with other dogs and experience new sights and sounds is an insurance policy to his growing up well adjusted, friendly and confident.
- Your pup's interactions with children must be supervised to make sure that they treat each other with respect.

Puppy Kindergarten

There's a good reason that Labrador Retrievers are among America's favorite canines. This is one smart fellow, an amiable guy who loves to learn and is easy to train. But the key word here is "train." He won't learn the house rules all by himself. A solid education in obedience and leadership is essential to teach your Lab how to behave in his new human world, and those lessons start the day you bring your puppy home.

All dogs are pack animals, and as such they need a leader. Your Lab's first boss was his dam, and all of his

The pup's first teacher is who else but Mom? Are you ready to take over the responsibility of pack leader?

life lessons came from his mom and littermates. When he played too rough or nipped too hard, his siblings cried and stopped the game. When he got pushy or unbearable, his dam cuffed him gently with a maternal paw or shook him by the scruff of the neck. Now you have to assume the role of leader and communicate appropriate behavior in terms his little canine mind will understand. Remember, too, that from a canine perspective, human rules make no sense at all.

It's no wonder that the Labrador is one of America's favorite breeds. Labs are gentle, friendly and easy-to-train dogs who respond well to positive reinforcement.

When you start the teaching process, keep this thought uppermost: the first 20 weeks of any canine's life are his most valuable learning time, a period when his mind is best able to soak up every lesson, both positive and negative. Positive experiences and proper socialization during this period are critical to his future development and stability. We've discussed the impor-

Your puppy is only this young once, and this is the age at which he is capable of learning the most quickly. Take advantage of his "sponge" stage and give him lots to absorb!

tance of socialization, so know this: the amount and quality of time you invest with your Labrador youngster now will determine what kind of an adult he will become. A wild dog or a gentleman or lady? A well-behaved or naughty dog? It's up to you!

Canine behavioral science tells us that any behavior that is rewarded will be repeated. That's called positive reinforcement. If something good happens, like a tasty treat or hugs and kisses, a puppy will naturally want to repeat the behavior. That same research also has proven that one of the best ways to a puppy's mind is through his stomach. Liver smells very pungent to your Labrador, so never underestimate the power of a liver snap! This leads to a very important puppy rule: keep your pockets loaded with puppy treats at all times so you are prepared to reinforce good behavior whenever it occurs.

That same reinforcement principle also applies to negative behavior, or what we humans might consider negative, like digging in the trash can, which the dog or puppy does not know is "wrong." If the pup gets into the garbage, steals food or does anything else that he thinks is fun or makes him feel good, he will do it again. Rewarding good behavior and correcting bad, at the time each occurs, teaches puppy right and wrong. "Catch him in the act" is the rule, so what better reason to keep a sharp eye on your puppy?

You are about to begin Puppy Training 101. Rule number one: the puppy must learn that you are now the "alpha dog" and his new pack leader. Rule number two: you have to teach him in a manner he will understand (sorry, barking just won't do it). Remember always that he knows nothing about human standards of behavior.

WORD ASSOCIATION

Use the same word (command) for each behavior every time you teach it, adding food rewards and verbal praise to reinforce the positive. The pup will make the connection and will be motivated to repeat the behavior when he hears those key words. For example, when he's urinating. Your pup will soon learn what those trips outside are for.

TIMING

All dogs learn their lessons in the present tense. You have to catch them in the act (good or bad) in order to dispense rewards or discipline. You have

Puppies are blank canvases and it's up to responsible owners to turn them into masterpieces.

teaching the pup to go potty outside, use the same potty term ("Go potty," "Get busy" and "Hurry up" are commonly used) each time he eliminates, adding a "Good boy!" while three to five seconds to connect with him or he will not understand what he did right or wrong. Thus, timing and consistency are your keys to success in teaching any new

CHAPTER 7

behavior or correcting bad behaviors.

Successful puppy training depends on several important principles:

1. Use simple one-word commands and say them only once. Otherwise,

something he did minutes earlier. Three to five seconds, remember?

3. Always praise (and offer a treat) as soon as he does something good (or when he stops doing something naughty). How else will

The use of food rewards has proven to be successful in introducing lessons and commands to your pup. What pup doesn't snap to attention at the sight of a tasty tidbit?

puppy learns that "Come" (or "Sit" or "Down") is a three- or four-word command.

2. Never correct your dog for

puppy know he's a good dog?

4. Be consistent. You can't snuggle together on the couch to watch TV today,

then scold him for climbing onto the couch tomorrow.

5. Never call your dog to you to correct him. This will defeat the come command in short order. He will think the correction is for coming to you, and why would he want to come to you if he is to be scolded? Always go to the dog to stop unwanted behavior, but be sure you catch him in the act or your correction will not be understood.

6. Never hit your dog or strike him with a newspaper or any other object. Such physical measures will only create fear and confusion in your dog and could provoke aggressive behavior down the road. Use your voice as your method of correction and keep your paws to yourself!

7. When praising or correcting, use your best doggie voice. Use a light and happy voice for praise and a firm, sharp voice for warnings or corrections. A whiny "No, No" or "Drop that" will not sound too convincing, nor will a deep, gruff voice that says "Good boy" make your puppy feel like having fun. Your dog also will respond accordingly to family arguments. If there's a shouting match, he will think that he did something wrong and head for cover. So never argue in front of the kids...or the dog!

PUPPY GAMES

Puppy games are great ways to entertain your puppy and yourself, while subliminally teaching lessons in the course of having fun. Start with a game plan and a pocketful of tasty dog treats. Keep your games short so you don't push his attention span beyond normal puppy limits. Labrador puppies love to have fun with their people. Games are excellent teaching aids and one of the best ways to say "I love you" to your puppy.

Find Your Toy: Start by placing one of his favorite toys in plain sight, and ask your puppy "Where's your toy?" and let him take it. Repeat several times. Then place your puppy safely outside the room and place the toy where only part of it shows. Bring him back and ask the same question. Praise highly when he finds it. Repeat several times. Finally, conceal the toy completely and let your puppy sniff it out. Trust his nose…he will find his toy.

Puppy Retrieve: This game helps teach the come com-

mand. With two people sitting on the floor about 10 or 15 feet apart, one person holds and pets the pup while the other calls him: "Puppy, puppy, come!" in a happy voice. When the pup comes running, lavish him with big hugs and give a tasty treat. Repeat back and forth several times, but don't overdo it. You can add a ball or toy and toss it back and forth for the puppy to retrieve. When he picks it up, praise and hug some more, give him a goodie to release the toy, then toss it back to person number two. Repeat as before.

Where's Your Daddy?: This is another game that teaches the puppy to "come." Play this game outdoors in your yard or other confined safe area. When the pup is distracted, hide behind a tree or bush. Shout out "Where's your dad?" (or whichever name you like). Peek out to see when he discovers you are gone and comes running back to find

Games of fetch are easy to teach—he's a retriever, remember? Simple games with your puppy will lead to formal retrieving when your Lab is an adult.

you (trust me, he will do that). As soon as he gets close, come out, squat down with arms outstretched and call him: "Puppy, come!" This is also an excellent bonding technique and teaches the puppy to depend on you.

DOGGY DAYCARE

The 21st-century Labrador Retriever, living in our busy world where both parents might work and the children are at school all day, can get pretty bored sitting at home, waiting for the family to return. Such a schedule could keep a family or a single owner from acquiring a dog in the first place. Fortunately, our modern world offers some options for busy owners in the form of doggy daycare.

These facilities are popping up all over the country, and smart dog owners are taking advantage of them. Doggy daycare centers not only offer your dog exercise but also provide stimulation and socialization for the budding Labrador student.

PUPPY KINDERGARTEN

Overview

- The Labrador is a bright and eager student, but he will only learn under your guidance.
- Take advantage of your pup's first 20 weeks, during which his aptitude for learning is greatest.
- Be consistent in your commands and in teaching your pup right from wrong.
- Timing is the key. You must catch puppy in the act to reinforce a correct behavior or correct an undesirable one.
- Understand and follow the basic principles of training.
- Use games to lead up to formal commands in a fun manner.
- Doggy daycare offers many benefits to today's busy dog owners.

CHAPTER 8

House-training Your Labrador

In the dog world, house-training and crate-training are almost synonymous terms. The dog crate is perhaps the most important piece of dog equipment you will buy, your Lab's personal "condo" that both of you will appreciate and enjoy. Because all canines are natural den creatures, thanks to the thousands of years their ancestors spent living in caves and cavities in the ground, your puppy will adapt quite naturally to crate confinement.

The crate is also a natural house-training aid. Your Lab puppy is an

Teaching proper toileting habits, meaning that your Labrador learns to use the outdoors for his potty needs, is an essential element of living happily with your dog.

inherently clean little fellow, and he will try hard not to soil his "den" or living space. Thus his crate is actually a multi-purpose dog accessory—your Lab's personal dog house within your house; a humane house-training tool; a security measure that will protect your dog, your household and your belongings when you're not home; a travel aid to house and protect your dog when you are traveling (most motels will accept a crated dog) and, finally, a comfy dog space for your Lab when your anti-dog relatives come to visit.

If training your pup to the back yard, you will guide him on-lead to the relief site you've chosen for him. After he's used it several times, he will follow his nose to the spot.

Some experienced breeders insist on crate use after their puppies leave, and a few even crate-train their pups before they send them home. But it's more likely that your pup has never seen a crate, so it's up to you to make sure his introduction to the crate is a pleasant one.

Introduce the crate as soon as he comes home so he learns that this is

"Can I have some privacy, please?" If you have a fenced yard, you can let your dog out on his own to do his business once he's learned to locate his toilet area.

his new "house." This is best accomplished with dog treats. For the first day or two, toss a tiny treat into the crate to entice him to go in. Pick a crate command, such as "Kennel," "Inside" or "Crate," and use it every time he enters. You also can feed his first few meals inside the crate with the door still open, so the crate association will be a happy one.

Your puppy should sleep in his crate from his very first night. He may whine at first and object to the confinement, but be strong and stay the course. If you release him when he cries, you provide his first life lesson: if I cry, I get out and maybe hugged. You can see why this not a good plan!

A better scheme is to place the crate next to your bed at night for the first few weeks. Your presence will comfort him, and you'll also know if he needs a midnight potty trip. Whatever you do, do not lend comfort by taking the puppy into bed with you. To a dog, on

the bed means equal, which is not a good idea this early in the game when you're establishing yourself as leader.

Make a practice of placing your puppy into his crate for naps, at nighttime and whenever you are unable to watch him closely. Not to worry, he will let you know when he wakes up and needs a potty trip. If he falls asleep under the table and wakes up when you're not there, guess what he'll do first?

Routines, consistency and an eagle eye are your keys to house-training success. Puppies always "go" when they wake up (quickly now!), within a few minutes after eating, after play periods and after brief periods of confinement. Most pups under 12 weeks of age will need to eliminate at least every hour or so, or up to 10 times a day (set your oven timer to remind you). Always take the puppy outside to the same area, telling him "Outside" as you go out. Pick a potty word ("Hurry up," "Go potty" and "Get busy" are the most commonly used) and use it when he does his business, lavishing him with "Good puppy!" praise and repeating your key word. Use the same exit door for these potty trips and confine puppy to the exit area so he can find it when he needs it. Watch for sniffing and circling or other signs that he has to relieve himself. Don't allow him to roam the house until he's house-trained; how will he find that outside door if he's three or four rooms away? He does not have a house map in his head.

Of course, he will have accidents. All puppies do. You wouldn't expect your toddler to suddenly not need diapers! Potty-training a child is actually considerably more difficult than housebreaking a Labrador puppy. Hmmm. Think about that! Humans take longer to learn to use the toilet than a puppy takes to figure out not to "go" on your carpet.

When you catch your pup

in the act indoors, clap your hands loudly, say "Aaah! Aaah!" and scoop him up to go outside. Your voice should startle him and make him stop. Be sure to praise when he finishes his duty outside.

This is a good sturdy crate to use with your Lab puppy as a travel crate and carrying case, providing him with a place of his own wherever you go.

If you discover the piddle spot after the fact…more than a few seconds later…you're too late. Pups only understand in the moment and will not understand a correction given more than five seconds (that's only five) after the deed. Correcting any later will only cause fear and confusion. Just forget it and vow to be more vigilant.

House-training hint: remove the puppy's water after 7 p.m. at night to aid in nighttime bladder control. If he gets thirsty, offer him an ice cube. Then just watch him race for the refrigerator when he hears the rattle of the ice cube tray.

Never rub your puppy's nose in his mistake or strike your puppy or adult dog with your hand, a newspaper or another object to correct him. He will not understand and will only become fearful of the person who is hitting him.

Despite its many benefits, crate use can be abused. Labrador Retriever puppies under 12 weeks of age should never be confined for more than two hours at a time, unless, of course, they are sleeping. A general rule of thumb is three hours maximum for a three-month-old pup, four to five hours for the four- or five-month-old and no more than six hours for dogs over six months of age. If you're unable to be home to release the dog, arrange for a relative, neighbor or dog-sitter to let him out to exercise and also go to the potty.

One final, but most important, rule of crate use: never, *ever*, use the crate for punishment. Successful crate use depends on your puppy's positive association with his "house." If the crate represents punishment, he will resist using it as his safe place. Sure, you can crate your pup after he has sorted through the trash to keep him confined while you clean up. Just don't do it in an angry fashion or tell him "Bad dog, crate!"

If you are crate-shy, what can you do with your uncrated puppy when you're not home? Confine him to one room with baby gates or another dog-proof barrier. Puppy-proof the room by removing anything the pup could chew or damage and hurt himself in the process. But even in a stripped environment, some pups will chew through drywall if bored. An exercise pen 4 feet by 4 feet square (available through pet suppliers), sturdy enough that pup can't knock it down, will provide safe containment for short periods. Paper one area for elimination, with perhaps a blanket in the opposite corner for napping. Safe chew toys should help keep him happy while you're gone.

Most importantly, remember that successful house-training revolves around consistency and repetition.

Maintain a strict schedule and use your key words consistently. Well-trained owners have well-trained pups.

This crate may be fine for your Lab puppy, but it won't be large enough for very long. It is recommended from the outset to purchase a crate that will accommodate the dog at his full size.

HOUSE-TRAINING YOUR LABRADOR

Overview

- When used correctly, the crate is an invaluable aid in house-training a puppy.
- Make your pup's introduction to the crate a positive one and never use the crate for punishment. You want your dog to think only happy thoughts when it comes to his crate.
- Set a potty routine and stick to it. Your puppy needs to go out very often, but the frequency of his relief trips will decrease as he gets older.
- Young puppies can't "hold it" for long, so keep an eye out for your pup's signals that he needs to go out. If accidents happen, it's more often the owner's fault than the pup's.
- Praise puppy when he goes where he should; that's how he will get the idea!
- Never punish a pup for accidents; just keep a closer watch on him to prevent accidents from happening.

Teaching Basic Commands

The Lab is a breed with much potential once he's learned basic good behavior. He can be trained to high levels of service; among the Lab's many uses is as an assistance dog for the handicapped, helping their owners perform everyday tasks.

All Labrador Retrievers have the potential to be well-behaved canine good citizens. They must learn good doggie manners if they are to be welcome wherever they go. They should be proficient, flawless in fact, in the commands such as come, sit, stay, down and heel. You can start your puppy's lessons as soon he comes home. Don't worry, he's not too young. This is his prime learning period, so the earlier you start, the easier the process and the more successful you both will be. Always start your teaching exercises in a quiet, distraction-free environment. Once your Lab pup has mastered any task, change the setting and practice in a different location and then with another person or a dog nearby. If the pup reacts to the new distraction and does not perform the exercise, take a step back and continue with the exercise by removing the distractions for a while.

Teaching new exercises is accomplished more easily with the help of a treat or two. A dog typically does not like assuming the down position on command, but when he follows a treat along the ground, he will be "getting down" before he knows it.

Appoint one person to instruct your puppy in the early stages so as not to confuse the pup. It's the too-many-cooks rule of dog training. Once your puppy has learned a command reliably, other family members can join in.

Ignore your Lab puppy for a few minutes before each training session. The lack of stimulation will make him more eager for your company and attention. Keep sessions short so your puppy won't get bored or lose his enthusiasm. In time, he will be

Despite being a water dog by nature, the Lab still needs a careful introduction to water, followed by training and practice to develop his innate skills.

able to concentrate for longer periods. Vary the exercises to keep his enthusiasm level high. Watch for signs of boredom and loss of attention—that's when you know it's time to stop.

Always keep your training lessons positive and upbeat. Use lots of praise, praise and more praise! Never train your puppy or adult dog if you are in a grumpy mood. You will lose patience, and he will think it is his fault. That will reverse any progress the two of you have made and create a negative association for future lessons.

Finish every training session on a positive note. If you have been struggling or unsuccessful, switch gears and do something he knows well (like sit!) to end the session.

Before you can effectively teach your puppy any command, two things must happen: Puppy must learn to respond to his name (name recognition) and you must be able to gain and hold his attention. How to accomplish that? Why, with treats, of course! Treats are defined as tiny tidbits, preferably something soft and easy to chew. We don't want to overfeed this pup. Thin slices of hotdogs cut into quarters work well.

Start by calling your Lab puppy's name. Once. Not two or three times, but once. Otherwise, he will learn that he has a three-part name and will ignore you when you say it once. Begin by using his name when he is undistracted and you are sure he will respond by looking at you, and pop him a treat as soon as he does. Repeat about a dozen times, several times a day. It won't take more than a day or so before he understands that his name means something good to eat.

A RELEASE COMMAND
You'll need a word to tell your dog that the exercise is over,

similar to "At ease" in the military. "All done" and "Free" are the ones most commonly recommended; "Okay" is also used. You'll need this release word so that your Lab will know that the exercise is finished and it's okay to relax and/or move from a stationary position.

TAKE IT AND LEAVE IT

Begin by placing a treat in the palm of your hand and saying "Take it" as your pup grabs the treat. Repeat three times. On the fourth time, do not say a word as your dog reaches for the treat; just close your fingers around the treat and wait. Do not pull away, but be prepared for the pup to paw, lick, bark and nibble on your fingers. Patience! When he finally pulls away from your hand and waits for a few seconds, open your hand and tell him "Take it." Repeat until he waits to "Take it."

Now the next step. Show your Lab the treat in the palm of your hand and tell him to "Leave it." When he goes for the treat, close your hand and repeat "Leave it." Repeat the process until he pulls away, then wait just a second, open your hand, tell him to "Take it" and allow him to take the treat. Repeat the "Leave it"

"Leave it" is necessary for a dog's safety, especially so with a curious Lab puppy who will investigate anything and everything with his mouth.

process until he waits just a few seconds, then give the treat on "Take it." Gradually extend the time that you wait after your puppy "Leaves it" and before you tell him to "Take it."

Now you want to teach your Lab to leave things on the ground, not just in your hand.

(Think of all the things you don't want him to pick up.) With your puppy on a loose leash, position yourself in front of him and toss a treat behind you and a little to the side so he can see it, while saying "Leave it." Here begins the dance. If he goes for the treat, use your body, not your hands, to block him, moving him backwards away from it. As soon as he backs off and gives up trying to get around you, unblock the treat and tell him "Take it." Be ready to block again if he goes for it before you give permission. Repeat the process until he understands and waits for the command.

Once your Lab knows this well, practice with his food dish, telling him to "Leave it," then "Take it" after he complies (he can either sit or stand while waiting for his dish). As before, gradually extend the waiting period before you tell him that it's okay to "Take it."

This reminds your Lab that you're the boss, you are in control, and that all good things, like food, come from the human who loves him. It will help prevent your puppy from becoming possessive of his food bowl, a behavior that only escalates and leads to more serious aggressive behaviors. The safety and good-behavior benefits of a solid Take it/Leave it are endless.

COME COMMAND
This command has life-saving potential, preventing your Lab from running into the street, chasing after a squirrel or otherwise "escaping" from you. Always practice the come command on-leash and in a safely confined area. You can't afford to risk failure or the pup will learn that he does not have to come when called, and his reliable response is essential.

Once you have the pup's attention, call him from a

short distance: "Puppy, come!" (use your happy voice) and give a treat when he comes to you. If he hesitates, tug him to you gently with his leash. Grasp and hold his collar with one hand as you dispense the treat. The collar grasp is important. You will eventually phase out the treat and switch to hands-on praise only. This maneuver also connects holding his collar with coming and treating, which will assist you in countless future behaviors.

Do 10 or 12 repetitions, 2 or 3 times a day. Once your pup has mastered the command, continue to practice daily to imprint this most important behavior onto his puppy brain. Experienced Lab owners know, however, that one can never *completely* trust a dog to come when called if the dog is bent on a self-appointed mission. Off-leash is often synonymous with out of control. Always keep your Labrador on a leash when not in a fenced or confined area.

SIT COMMAND

This one's a snap, since your Lab already understands the treating process. Stand in front of your pup, move the treat directly over his nose and slowly move it backwards over his head. As he folds backwards to reach the goodie, his rear will move downward to the floor. If the puppy raises up to reach the treat, just lower it a bit. The moment his behind is down, tell him "Sit." Release the

Guide your Lab into the sit position with a gentle push on his rump and he'll get the idea after a few tries. The sit is an easy exercise to teach.

treat and gently grasp the collar as you did with "Come." He will again make that positive connection between the treat, the sit position, and the collar hold.

As he becomes more proficient, make him hold the sit position longer before you give the treat (this is the beginning of the stay command). Begin using your release word to release him

Start teaching the sit/stay just a short distance from the dog, with him on lead. Use your hand as a stay signal along with the word "stay."

from the sit position. Practice using the sit command for everyday activities such as sitting for his food bowl or a toy, and do random sits

throughout the day, always for a food or praise reward. Once he is reliable, combine the "Sit" and "Leave it" for his food dish.

STAY COMMAND

"Stay" is really just an extension of "Sit," which your Lab already knows. With puppy sitting when commanded, place the palm of your hand in front of his nose and tell him "Stay." Count to five. Give him his release word to end the stay and praise him. Stretch out the stays in tiny increments, making allowances for puppy energy.

Once he stays reliably, move your body a step backwards after giving the command, then step forward again. Gradually extend the time and distance that you move away. If puppy moves, say "No" and move in front of him. Use sensible timelines, depending on your puppy's attention span.

DOWN COMMAND

The down command can be a tough one to master. Because the down is a submissive posture, some Labs and certain take-charge breeds may find it especially difficult. That's why it's most important to teach it when they're very young.

From the sit position, move the food lure from his nose to the ground and slightly backwards between his front paws. Wiggle it as necessary to spark his interest. As soon as his front legs and rear end hit the floor, give the treat and tell him "Down, good boy, down!" thus connecting the word to the behavior. "Down" may prove difficult, so be patient and generous with the praise when he cooperates. Once he goes into the down position with ease, incorporate the stay as you did with the sit. By six months of age, your puppy should be able to do a ten-minute solid sit/say, ditto for a down/stay.

WAIT COMMAND

You'll love this one, especially when your Lab comes into the house with wet or muddy paws. Work on the wait command with a closed interior door. (It would not be wise to try this with an outside-exit door.) Start to open the door as if to go through or out. When your dog tries to follow, step in front and body-block him to prevent his passage. Don't use the word "wait" just yet. Keep blocking until he hesitates and you can open the door a little to pass through. Then say your wait release word, "Through" or "Okay" or whatever release word you have chosen for this exercise, and let him go through the door. Repeat by body-blocking until he understands and waits for you, then start applying the "Wait" command to the behavior. Practice in different doorways, progressing to outside entrances once he will wait reliably.

HEEL COMMAND

A young Lab should be taught simply to walk politely on a leash, at or near your side. That is best accomplished when your pup is very young and small, before he can pull you down the street! The formal "heel" will come later.

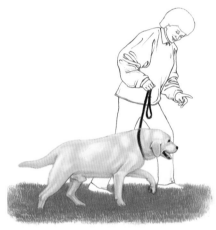

You'll be spending a lot of time walking with your Lab. A heel-trained dog with whom you can enjoy your walks is a much better option than being dragged down the street!

Start leash training soon after your pup comes home. Simply attach his leash to his buckle collar and let him drag it around for a little while every day. Play a puppy game with the leash on. Make wearing his leash a happy moment in his day. If he chews the leash, distract him with a play activity. You also can deter chewing by spraying the leash with a bitter product to make it taste unpleasant.

After a few days, gather up the leash in a distraction-free zone of the house or yard and take just a few steps together. With your puppy on your left side, hold a treat lure at his eye level to encourage him to walk next to you. Pat your knee and use a happy voice. Say "Let's go!" as you move forward, holding the treat low to keep him near. Take a few steps, give the treat and praise! Move forward just a few steps each time.

Keep these sessions short and happy, a mere 30 seconds at a time (that's long in puppy time). Never scold or nag him into walking faster or slower, just encourage him with happy talk. Walk straight ahead at first, adding wide turns once he gets the hang of it. Progress to 90° turns, using a gentle leash tug on the turns, a happy verbal "Let's go!" and, of course, a treat. Walk in short 10- to 20-second bursts with a happy break (use your release word) and brief play (nothing wild or crazy, hugs will do nicely) in between. Keep total training time short and always quit with success, even if just a few short steps.

A FEW MORE TIPS

All of these behaviors are taught in some phase of a young-dog training class. Check with your vet or a local kennel club to find one in your area. There are dozens of books written on positive training methods. Clubs may also hold special training seminars. Learn all you can. You and your Lab will both be smarter for your efforts.

Ongoing practice is actually a lifetime dog rule, especially for a strong-willed dog. Dogs will be dogs and, if we don't maintain their skills, they will sink back into sloppy, inattentive behaviors that will be harder to correct. Incorporate these commands into your daily routine and your Labrador Retriever will remain a polite gentleman or lady of whom you can be proud.

TEACHING BASIC COMMANDS

Overview

- A solid foundation in the basic commands is the basis of your Labrador's becoming a well-mannered canine citizen.
- Before beginning any lesson, your pup must recognize his name and you must be able to get and keep his attention.
- "Take it" and "Leave it" help you control what goes into your orally fixated Lab's mouth.
- The basic commands include come, sit, stay, down, heel and wait.
- Make practice part of your daily routine to keep your Lab sharp and reliable. You will find many opportunities each day to reinforce your dog's knowledge of the commands he's learned.

CHAPTER 10

Home Care for Your Labrador

The average Labrador Retriever lives for 10 to 13 years. The quality of those years depends on a conscientious home health-care program. Although genetics and the environment certainly can influence a dog's longevity, the fact remains that you are the backbone of your Labrador's health-maintenance program. Like the proverbial apple-a-day, your daily focus on canine wellness will help "keep the vet away."

Labs who are fed properly and kept active should have no problem maintaining healthy weight and condition.

WEIGHT CONTROL

If your Labrador could suddenly speak, the first thing that he would say is "Who are you calling a chow-hound?" No Lab has ever been accused of having a poor appetite! To determine whether your Labrador is overweight, you should be able to feel your dog's ribs beneath a thin layer of muscle with very gentle pressure on his rib cage. When viewing your dog from above, you should be able to see a definite waistline; from the side, he should have an obvious tuck-up in his abdomen. Lean is healthier, as obesity can take two to three years off a dog's life.

Labs have the tendency to become too stocky if they do not get enough exercise or if they are allowed to overeat. It's a rare Labrador who will turn down a tasty morsel!

Keep a record of his weight from each annual vet visit. A few extra pounds? Adjust his food portions (always avoid table scraps), perhaps switch to a lower-calorie dog-food formula and increase his exercise.

A Lab in fit condition will give an overall impression of athleticism and agility, showing good musculature.

Excessive weight is especially hard on older dogs with creaky joints. A senior Lab who is sedentary will grow out of shape more quickly. Walking and running (slower for old guys) are still the best workouts for health maintenance. Tailor your dog's exercise to fit his age and physical condition.

CHECKING OVER THE COAT

Your weekly grooming sessions should include body checks for lumps (cysts, warts and fatty tumors), hot spots and other skin or coat problems. While harmless skin lumps are common in older dogs, many can be malignant, and your vet should examine any abnormality. Black mole-like patches or growths on any body part require immediate veterinary inspection. Remember, petting and hugging can also turn up little abnormalities.

Be extra-conscious of dry skin, a flaky coat and thinning hair, all signs of possible thyroid disease. Check for fleas and flea dirt (especially on your dog's underside and around the base of the tail) if you think fleas could be present.

EYE CARE

Your Labrador's vision may deteriorate with age. A bluish haze to the eyes is common in geriatric dogs and does not impair vision, but you should always check with your vet about any changes in the eyes to determine if these are harmless or indicative of a problem.

THE OTHER END

Don't forget your dog's backside. Does he chew at his rear or scoot and rub it on the carpet? That's a sign of impacted anal glands. Have your vet express those glands. (It's not a job for amateurs.) Have annual stool cultures done to check for intestinal parasites; hook-, whip- and roundworms can cause weight and appetite loss, poor coat quality and all manner of intestinal problems, which can weaken your dog's resistance to other canine diseases. See your vet if any of those signs appear. Tapeworms, a common parasite that comes from fleas, look like grains of rice tucked in the stool.

and changes in sleeping habits. Heart disease can be treated if you catch it early.

KIDNEY DISEASE
Kidney disease also can be treated successfully with early

All dogs enjoy a good roll in the grass, but who knows what kinds of unwanted passengers may have jumped aboard in the process? Check his skin and coat regularly, particularly after romps in grassy or wooded areas.

HEART DISEASE
Heart disease is common in all canines, yet it is one that dog owners most frequently overlook. Symptoms include panting and shortness of breath, chronic coughing, especially at night or upon first waking in the morning,

diagnosis. Dogs seven years and older should be tested annually for kidney and liver function. If your dog drinks excessive amounts of water and urinates more frequently, or has accidents in the house, run, don't walk, to your vet. Kidney disease can be managed with special diets to reduce the workload on the kidneys.

DOGGY EMERGENCIES

For everyday commonsense care, every dog owner should know the signs of an emergency. Many dog agencies, humane societies and animal shelters sponsor canine first-aid seminars. Participants learn how to recognize and deal with signs of common emergency situations, how to assemble a first-

Heatstroke is a concern for dogs, so ensure that your dog has plenty of drinking water, access to shade and a place to cool off.

aid kit, how to give CPR to a dog and more.

Vomiting for more than 24 hours, bloody or prolonged (over 24 hours) diarrhea, fever (normal canine temperature is 101.5) or a sudden swelling of the head or any body part (allergic reaction to an insect bite or other stimulus) are signs of serious problems. Symptoms of other common emergency situations include:

Heatstroke: Excessive panting, drooling, rapid pulse, dark reddened gums and a frantic, glazed expression (you'll know it when you see it).

Hypothermia (wet dogs + cold weather): Shivering, very pale gums and body temperature under 100 degrees.

Shock: Severe blood loss from an injury can send a dog into shock. Symptoms include shivering, weak pulse, weakness and listlessness, depression and lowered body temperature.

Other symptoms: Additional red flags for cancer or other serious health problems include: lumps or abnormal swelling; sores that do not heal; sudden or unexplainable weight loss; loss of appetite; unexplained bleeding or discharge; an offensive body odor; difficulty swallowing or eating; loss of stamina or reluctance to exercise; difficulty breathing, urinating or defecating; a bloated appearance; persistent stiffness or lameness.

Call your vet at once if you notice any of these warning signs. Many canine diseases and some cancers are treatable if they are diagnosed in the early stages.

The moral here is: know your Lab. Early detection is the key to your dog's longevity and quality of life. Cultivate a keen awareness of even subtle changes in your dog. Read books on canine health care and first aid and add one to your library. Keep a list of symptoms and remedies and your vet's emergency number in a handy place. Your Lab's life could depend on it.

HOME CARE FOR YOUR LABRADOR

Overview

- Your focus on home care for your Lab should be on maintenance of good health and prevention of illness.
- A dog's proper weight contributes directly to his health, longevity and quality of life.
- Use grooming sessions and regular petting to check your dog's coat and skin for any signs of problems.
- Care of your dog's eyes and anal sacs and being aware of his heart and kidney health, along with parasite control, are key elements of a comprehensive home-care routine.
- Be prepared for doggy emergencies by having a well-stocked first aid kit, recognizing the symptoms and keeping your vet's number close at hand.

Feeding Your Labrador Retriever

To keep your Labrador Retriever in prime condition, you should feed him a quality food that is appropriate for his age and lifestyle. Only a top-quality food will provide the proper balance of the vitamins, minerals and fatty acids that are necessary to support healthy bone, muscle, skin and coat.

The premium dog-food manufacturers have developed their formulas with strict quality controls. The labels on the food bags tell you what

To start, continue feeding your puppy the same diet he was fed by the breeder. The breeder will likely give you a few days' supply of food for the puppy; if you wish to feed a different food, changes should be made gradually.

products are in the food (beef, chicken, corn, etc.), and list ingredients in descending order of weight or amount in the food. Do not add your own supplements, "people food" (some, like chocolate, onions, grapes and nuts, are actually toxic to dogs) or extra vitamins to the food. You will only upset the nutritional balance of the food, which could affect the growth or maintenance of your Lab, or make him ill.

Lab puppies don't need to be told twice that it's dinnertime!

The major dog-food brands now offer foods for every size, age and activity level. As with human infants, puppies require a diet different from that of an adult. Puppy growth formulas contain protein and fat levels that are appropriate for the different-sized breeds. Large-breed, fast-growing dogs like Labradors require less protein and fat during these early months of rapid growth, which is better for healthy joint development. Medium and small

Treats are very helpful aids in puppy training, but the calories can add up quickly. Don't forget to factor in treats when figuring your dog's daily food portion to avoid overfeeding.

Labrador Retriever

breeds likewise have different nutritional requirements during their first year of growth.

In the world of quality dog foods, there are enough choices to confuse even experienced dog folks. Don't be intimidated by all those dog foods on the store shelves. Read the labels on the containers (how else can you learn what's in those foods?) and call the manufacturer's information number to learn more. Ask your breeder and your vet which food they recommend for your Lab pup. A solid education in the dog-food business will provide the tools you need to offer your dog a diet that is best for his long-term health.

If you plan to switch from the food fed by your breeder, take home a small supply of the breeder's food to mix with your own. Make the change gradually to aid your puppy's adjustment to his new food.

Now let's consider how many times to feed your puppy. An eight-week-old puppy does

best eating three times a day. At about 12 weeks of age, you can switch to twice-daily feedings. Most breeders suggest two meals a day for the life of the dog, regardless of breed, rather than one large one.

On the subject of when to serve meals, most owners agree that scheduled meals are preferable to free-feeding (that is, leaving the bowl out all day). Scheduled meals give you one more opportunity to remind your Labrador that all good things in life come from you— his master and chef. With scheduled meals, it's also easier to predict elimination, which is the better road to house-training. Regular meals help you know just how much your puppy eats and when, which is valuable information for weight control and noticing appetite changes that could signal illness. Further, most often free-feeding fosters picky eating habits...a bite here, a nibble there. Free-feeders are also more likely to become possessive of their food bowls, a problem behavior that signals the beginning of aggression.

Should you feed canned or dry food, offer the dry food with or without water? Dry food is recommended by most vets, since the dry particles help clean the dog's teeth of plaque and tartar. Adding water to dry food is optional. The Lab will do better with a splash of water in his food pan to prevent him from "inhaling" his food, as gulping food is a contributor to the deadly condition known as bloat, which affects deep-chested dogs. A bit of water added immediately before eating is also thought to enhance the flavor of the food, while still preserving the dental benefits. Whether feeding wet or dry, water should be available, although it is also thought a good bloat preventative to limit water intake at mealtimes.

Like people, puppies and adult dogs have different appetites; some will lick their food bowls clean and beg for more, while others pick at their food and leave some of it untouched. It's easy to overfeed a chow hound. Who can resist those soulful Labrador eyes? Be strong and stay the right course! Chubby puppies may be cute and cuddly, but the extra weight will stress their growing joints and is thought to be a factor in

Your puppy requires a different diet from that of an adult. Your Lab puppy needs a quality diet designed to promote healthy growth in large-breed dogs.

the development of hip and elbow disease. Overweight pups also tend to grow into over-weight adults who tire easily and will be more susceptible to other health problems. Consult your breeder and your vet for advice on how to adjust meal portions as your puppy grows.

Always remember that lean is healthy, fat is not. Research

has proven that obesity is a major canine killer. Quite simply, a lean dog lives longer than one who is overweight. And that doesn't even reflect the better quality of life for the lean dog that can run, jump and play without the burden of an extra 10 or 20 pounds.

To complicate the dog-food dilemma, there are also raw foods available for those who prefer to feed their dogs a completely natural diet rather

Labrador Retrievers who are active in field and water work will require a different diet than those who get less exercise. Discuss these dietary needs with your vet.

than traditional manufactured dog food. The debate on raw and/or all-natural vs. manufactured dog food is a fierce one, with some raw-food proponents claiming that raw diets have cured their dogs' allergies and other chronic ailments. If you are interested in this alternative feeding method, there

are various books on the topic, written by canine nutrition experts. You also can check with your vet, ask your breeder, surf the Internet and talk to dog owners who've had success with a raw diet.

If your adult dog is overweight, you can switch to a "light" food, which has fewer calories and more fiber. "Senior" foods for older dogs have formulas designed to meet the needs of less active older dogs. "Performance" diets contain more fat and protein for dogs that compete in sporting disciplines or lead very active lives.

Before closing, we must discuss bloat futher. This condition causes a dog's stomach to twist on itself, preventing exit of gas and cutting off blood flow, leading to shock and death if not treated immediately. Some theories suggest that gulping large amounts of food or drinking copious amounts of water right after eating can contribute to the condition.

Other bloat-prevention measures include no heavy exercise for at least an hour before eating and two hours afterwards. Make sure your dog is not overly excited during meals; it is also believed that nervous and overly excited dogs are more prone to this life-threatening condition. Symptoms include unproductive attempts to vomit and relieve himself, drooling and obvious discomfort.

Discuss the preventatives and the symptoms with your vet so that you can get your dog to the clinic right away if you suspect bloat.

The bottom line is this: what and how much you feed your dog are major factors in his overall health and longevity. It's worth your investment in extra time and dollars to provide the best diet for your dog.

FEEDING YOUR LABRADOR RETRIEVER

Overview

- Your Lab needs a balanced complete diet designed for large-breed dogs. He will start off on a good puppy food, then switch to adult-maintenance food and possibly change to a senior diet as he gets older.
- Discuss with your vet and breeder the correct amount to feed your Lab to maintain him in good condition, as obesity is detrimental to a dog's health and can shorten his lifespan.
- Stick to a daily feeding schedule of two meals per day; free-feeding is not recommended.
- The deep-chested Lab is one of the breeds prone to bloat. Learn to prevent your dog from becoming affected and to recognize symptoms.
- Your Labrador's health, coat quality, activity level and overall condition depend on his diet.

CHAPTER 12

Grooming Your Labrador

Good grooming habits are important for your dog's physical well-being and should be a weekly process.

Introduce the brush, nail clippers and toothbrush when he is just a pup. Dogs who have not experienced these ministrations early in life may object when they are older, bigger and better able to resist.

Start with tiny increments of time, stroking your pup gently with a soft brush, briefly handling his paws, looking inside his ears, gently touching his gums. Use lots of sweet talk and offer little treats.

Dental care is an important part of your dog's overall home health-care regimen and should be a regular part of your grooming routine.

The adult Labrador has a short and straight double coat, with an undercoat that varies in density depending on the climate in which he is raised. Weekly brushing will remove dust and distribute the oils that keep his coat clean and conditioned, with more frequent brushing needed during shedding season.

Labrador Retrievers of all colors possess short, straight, dense coats that are somewhat hard to the touch, along with undercoats to protect them from the elements.

Frequent bathing is seldom necessary and, in fact, will remove essential oils from your dog's skin and coat. Frequent brushing is the best way to remove dust and distribute those oils to keep his coat in super sheen.

How often should you bathe your Labrador? In most cases, no more than once every month or two. Of course, there are those times when a bath is necessary. To minimize the stress and struggle of bath time, start when your pup is small. Lure your puppy into the tub with treats. Line the tub or shower with a towel or mat for safe footing. Start with a dry tub, and after pup is

This is most Labradors' idea of getting cleaned up!

comfortable there, gradually add shallow water and the bathing process.

After shampooing, be sure to rinse the coat completely to avoid any itching from residual shampoo. A good chamois is the ideal tool for drying, as it absorbs water like a sponge. Keep him away from drafts for a good while after bathing and drying to prevent chilling. Spritz-on dry shampoos are handy in case you need a quick clean-up to remove dirt or odor.

Dental hygiene is as important for canines as it is for humans. Plaque and tartar build-up can lead to gum disease, which is a harbinger of more serious diseases of the internal organs.

A daily toothbrushing is the ideal, but twice weekly may be more realistic. Start the process while he is a pup and use positive associations like petting and praise. Begin by just rubbing your finger around his gums and over his puppy teeth. Graduate to a doggie toothbrush or simply use a gauze pad wrapped around your index finger. Canine toothpaste will enhance the process; "people" paste will make him sick.

Home dental care is vital to your Lab's health and longevity. Studies prove that good oral hygiene can add three to five years to a dog's life. Need we say more?

Nails should be trimmed once a month, but this is always the least favorite grooming chore. Puppies naturally do not like pedicures, so start nail clipping as soon as possible. Try to make it a positive experience. Offer those puppy treats with each clipping lesson. Thus will your puppy learn that when you touch his paws or trim those nails, he will receive a food reward. Yum!

At first you may have to settle on only one or two nails at a time. It is better to trim a small amount of nail more frequently than to try to cut back a nail that has grown too long. Nip off the nail tip or clip at the curved part of the nail. Be careful not to cut the quick (the pink vein in the nail), as that is quite painful, and the nail may bleed profusely. If you happen to snip a quick, you can stanch the bleeding with a few drops of a clotting solution or a styptic stick.

Weekly ear checks are worth the proverbial pound of cure. The Labrador's floppy ears can prevent air flow and keep the ear canals moist and ripe for musty growths. Some dogs also tend to accumulate more ear wax than others. Regular cleansing, especially after

swimming, with a specially formulated ear cleanser obtained through your veterinarian, will keep your dog's ears clean and odor-free. Use a cotton ball or wipe to clean the folds of the upper ear, but do not probe inside to avoid damaging the eardrum.

Symptoms of ear infection include redness and/or swelling of the ear flap or inner ear, a nasty odor or a dark, waxy discharge. If your Lab digs at his ear(s), shakes his head a lot or appears to lose his balance, see your vet at once.

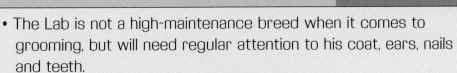

GROOMING YOUR LABRADOR

Overview

- The Lab is not a high-maintenance breed when it comes to grooming, but will need regular attention to his coat, ears, nails and teeth.
- Start all aspects of the grooming routine when your Lab is a pup so that he doesn't resist these procedures as an adult.
- The Lab's short double coat only needs regular brushing, and bathing as the need arises, to keep his coat in super sheen.
- Make toothbrushing part of your Lab's grooming sessions for a healthy mouth and teeth.
- Trim nails monthly with nail clippers made for dogs.

Keeping Your Lab Active

T he Labrador Retriever was originally bred to hunt. Even though the 21st-century Lab is more pet than hunter, he still hears the same ancestral call and needs vigorous exercise and activities to channel all that innate energy. You, the owner, will benefit as well, since a well-exercised dog is happily tired and less inclined to find mischievous outlets for his unexpended energy.

That said, bear in mind that neither the Lab puppy nor adult will get proper exercise on his own. He needs a reason or incentive to keep

The trainable and athletic Lab has achieved high levels of success in obedience competition. This illustration shows retrieving over a jump, which is an advanced exercise.

moving, and that incentive is, of necessity, the person in charge—you! A brisk daily walk or, better yet, two walks a day, will help keep your Labrador fit and trim while also keeping his mind stimulated through the sights and sounds of street life or the neighborhood park.

Your Lab will enjoy working off some energy with an exercise partner.

DOG WALKS

How long and how far to walk depends on your Lab's age, his physical condition and his energy level. A young Labrador's bones are softer and more vulnerable to injury during his first year of life and should not be subjected to heavy stress. That means shorter walks and no games or activities that encourage jumping or heavy impact on his front or rear until your pup is past the danger age. Playtime with other puppies and older dogs should be supervised to avoid excessive wrestling and twisting until your pup's structure has matured.

A day at the beach, retrieving in the surf with his friends—and a Labrador will be as happy as a clam!

Swimming, whenever possible, is excellent exercise—give him the chance to paddle those energetic feet.

When and where to walk are as important as how long. On warm days, avoid walking during midday heat and go out during the cooler morning or evening hours. If you're a jogger, your adult Lab buddy is the perfect running partner if he is in good physical condition. Jogging on turf or other soft surface is easier on your Lab's joints and feet. Just make sure that your dog is healthy and fully developed before joining you on your daily run.

Walks with your Labrador also provide excellent bonding time. Your Lab will look forward eagerly to his special time with you. As a creature of habit, your dog will bounce with joy when he sees you don your cap, pick up his leash or rattle your house keys.

OBEDIENCE CLASS

Consider taking your exercise program to another level. Plan a weekly night out with your Labrador and enroll in a class. Obedience, maybe agility…or both! The benefits of obedience class are endless. You will be motivated to work with your dog daily so you don't look unprepared or unraveled at each week's class. You'll both be more active and thus healthier. Your dog will learn the basics of obedience, will be better behaved and will become a model citizen. As an added benefit, he will discover that you really are the boss!

AGILITY CLASS

Agility class offers even more healthy outlets for Labrador energy. He will learn to scale an A-frame ramp, race headlong through a tunnel, balance himself on a teeter-totter, jump onto and off a platform, jump through a hoop, zigzag between a row of posts and more. Agility training should not start until at least 12 months of age. When starting out, keep jump heights very low and work surfaces of a resilient material to limit impact on the youngster's bones and muscles. Learning to navigate these agility obstacles, and your Lab's success in mastering them, will make you proud of both of you!

COMPETITION

You can take both of these activities one step further and participate with your dog in obedience and agility competitions. Shows and trials are held year-round and are designed for all levels of experience. Find a club or join a training group. Working with other Labrador fanciers will give you the incentive to keep working with your dog. Check with your Labrador Retriever breed club and the AKC for details and contact people.

HUNT TESTS AND HUNTING

What better way to exercise and enjoy your Lab than doing what most Labs love best—retrieving ducks and pheasants! A Labrador's love of bird work can range from

When you and your Lab are out and about, he can be a helper by carrying his own light pack.

mild to wildly passionate, depending on his working ancestry, but almost every Lab will enjoy time spent working in the field. Both the American Kennel Club (AKC) and the United Kennel Club (UKC) sponsor hunt tests, which are designed for the non-competitive sportsman who may or may not actually hunt. Your local breed or retriever club can refer you to groups who train specifically for such events. Rules and regulations for hunt tests are available on the AKC's and UKC's websites.

FIELD TRIALS

By far the most challenging and difficult of all sporting dog events, field trials are for those stout hearts who have the time and money to compete against the very best. Labradors dominate the field-trial scene, with dozens of Labs earning field championships every year. But pedigree is the name of this

If you have a show-quality puppy, give conformation competition a try to see where it leads. This dog has made it to the most prestigious show in the US, as he is being judged in the breed ring at the Westminster Kennel Club show.

game. Make sure you have a pup with outstanding credentials before you consider entering the field-trial world.

DOG SHOWS

Conformation is by far the most popular canine competition activity for all breeds. If you plan to show your Labrador, make sure you look for a show-quality puppy and discuss your goals with the breeder. Many local clubs host conformation training classes and can help novices get started with their pups. It's best to start show training when your Lab is young so he develops a good ring attitude.

YOUR LAB'S FAVORITE PLAYMATE—YOU!

Competition aside, your Lab will be happiest when he is with people, especially his owners. He needs to be part of family activities, he loves to play with the kids and he will be an eager participant in outdoor sports and indoor play. If any single word befits the Lab, it's *family*.

KEEPING YOUR LAB ACTIVE

Overview

- With such a versatile dog, you and your Lab have so many ways in which you can stay active.
- Your Lab needs at least two good walks each day to stay fit and mentally stimulated.
- Consider an obedience or agility class; from there, you can progress to the competitive level if you wish.
- The Lab will enjoy honing his instinctive skills in hunt tests or even the very competitive field trials if you are up to the challenge.
- If you obtained a show-quality pup, you can train for and compete in conformation.

LABRADOR RETRIEVER

Your Labrador and His Vet

A good veterinarian is the foundation of your Labrador's health-care program. Find a good vet before you bring your puppy home. Ask your friends, check with the local kennel club and your breeder. A good vet will plan your puppy's long-term health care and help you become smarter about canine health-care issues.

Take your puppy to your veterinarian within three or four days after you bring him home. Show the vet any health records of

Discuss with your vet the safest and most prudent course of protection for your puppy with regard to his inoculations.

shots and wormings from your breeder. He will conduct a thorough physical exam to make sure your Lab pup is in good health and will work out a schedule for vaccinations, microchipping, routine medications and regular well-puppy visits. A good vet will be gentle and affectionate with a new pup and do everything possible to make sure the puppy is not frightened.

By nursing from their mother, the litter receives nutrition plus immunity to certain diseases for their first weeks of life. This antibiotic colostrum is found only in mother's milk.

Vaccine protocol for puppies varies with many veterinarians, but most recommend a series of three "combination" shots given at three-to-four week intervals. Your puppy should have had his first shot before he left his breeder. "Combination" shots vary, and a single injection may contain five, six, seven or even eight vaccines in one shot. Many breeders and veterinarians feel the potency in high-combination vaccines can negatively compromise a puppy's immature immune system, so they

Your vet will assess your Lab's teeth, mouth and gums at each checkup. Keep your dog smiling in between veterinary visits with attention to his dental care at home.

recommend fewer vaccines in one shot or even separating vaccines into individual shots.

VACCINES

The vaccines recommended by the American Veterinary Medical Association (AVMA) are called CORE vaccines, those which protect against diseases most dangerous to your puppy and adult dog. These include: distemper, fatal in puppies; canine parvovirus, highly contagious and also fatal in puppies and at-risk dogs; canine adenovirus, highly contagious and high risk for pups under 16 weeks of age; canine hepatitis, highly contagious, pups at high risk. Rabies immunization is required in all 50 states.

Non-CORE vaccines no longer routinely recommended by the AVMA, except when the risk is present, are canine parainfluenza, leptospirosis, canine coronavirus, Bordetella (canine cough) and Lyme disease (borreliosis). Your vet will alert you if your pup should be protected from these.

Research suggests that annual vaccinations may actually be over-vaccinating and may be responsible for many of today's canine health problems. Mindful of that, it is strongly suggested that veterinarians and owners consider a dog's individual needs and exposure before they decide on a vaccine protocol. Many dog owners now have annual titer tests done to check their dog's antibodies rather than automatically vaccinating.

Always ask your vet what shots or medications your dog is getting at each visit and what they are for. A well-informed dog owner is better prepared to raise a healthy dog. Keep a notebook or dog diary, and record all health information, especially after every vet visit, so you won't forget it. Believe me, you will forget!

FLEAS AND TICKS

Fleas have been around for centuries, and it's likely that you will wage flea battle sometime during your Lab's lifetime. Fortunately today there are several low-toxic, effective flea weapons to aid you in your flea war.

These products can kill fleas and ticks for 30 to 90 days (or more). Some items are spot-on treatments that can be applied between the shoulder blades and others are monthly pills. The best remedies are available through your veterinarian. Over-the-counter flea and tick collars offer only limited protection and are risky at best.

Tick-borne diseases such as Lyme disease (canine borreliosis), ehrlichiosis and Rocky Mountain spotted fever are now found in almost every state and can affect humans as well as dogs. Dogs that live in or visit areas where ticks are present,

whether seasonally or year-round, should be protected.

BE AWARE OF CHANGES

Your Lab's health is in your hands between his annual visits to the vet. Be ever-conscious of any changes in his appearance or behavior. Things to consider:

A happy seven-month-old, in good health and off to a great start!

- Has your Lab gained a few too many pounds or suddenly lost weight?
- Are his teeth clean and white?
- Is he urinating more frequently, drinking more water than usual?
- Does he strain during a bowel movement?
- Any changes in his appetite?
- Does he appear short of breath, lethargic, overly tired?
- Have you noticed limping or joint stiffness?

These are all signs of serious health problems that you should discuss with your vet as soon as they appear. This is especially important for the senior dog, since even minor changes can be a sign of something serious.

SPAY/NEUTER?

This is almost a non-question, since spaying/neutering is the best health insurance policy you can give your Labrador.

Statistics prove that females spayed before their first heat cycle (estrus) have 90% less risk of several common female cancers and other serious female health problems. Males neutered before their male hormones kick in, usually before six months of age, enjoy zero to greatly reduced risk of testicular and prostate cancer and other related tumors and infections. Statistically, you will be helping both the pet overpopulation problem and your dog's long-term health.

YOUR LABRADOR AND HIS VET

Overview

- Find a skilled vet in your area and have an appointment set up before bringing your puppy home.
- At the first visit, your vet will set up your pup's vaccination schedule. Opinions vary about the best vaccination protocol, so discuss with your vet the safest way to inoculate.
- Parasite control is a must. Most every dog owner faces pests like fleas and ticks at some time in their dogs' lives.
- Know your Lab! Be aware of changes in his appearance and/or behavior, as these could be indicative of something serious, and call the vet right away.
- Spaying/neutering protects your dog from many types of cancer and other serious problems.